# Cosmic Wilderness

To Eve,

We extend our greatest
gratitude and love to
You and the fire You keep.

May God Bless You
And Goddess Protect You
Always!


Matthew and Pooja

Published by Rose Gold Publishing, LLC
Cover design by Pooja Bakhai
Interior photos by Pooja Bakhai and Matthew Steele

Printed in the United States of America.

ISBN: 978-1-952070-61-7

www.rosegoldpublishingllc.com

# ACKNOWLEDGEMENTS

*For all those who walk the path...*

*to the fire and back again.*

*Gratitude to pachamama,*
*the divine,*
*our soul families, birth families,*
*the guardians of the land*
*and*
*the keepers of the spirits*

*thank you*
*thank you*
*thank you*

*To my Beloved (Be-Loved),*

*You are my world, my best friend. You are my truest confidant and mirror, my greatest teacher in whom I admire deeply. Your inspiration, compassion and love—I can only hope to be half of who and what you are.*

*An ode to our future children, truly I am honored and filled with joy, for you have the best mother. For my part in these love reminders, sometimes, I am doing the reminding and other times, I am being reminded.*

*Greetings beloved,*

*It is an honor meeting you once again.*
*As everything continues to fall apart,*
*let us hold on to each other,*
*hold space for each other,*
*share our medicine,*
*and dream up*
*the most beautiful revolution possible.*

# INTRODUCTION

Before we met in the Amazon jungles of Ecuador, I was on the Zhuracpamba mountain. Zhuracpamba translates to 'mountain of thorns.' I was engaged in my vision quest upon this mountain, surrounded by my prayers and the wild horses that kept me company at night. Pooja was enjoying the beauty of Mexico, exploring beaches by day and dancing by night. Little did we know what the continuation of our journeys had in store for us. Though we both knew this type of union was possible, we took very different yet divinely similar paths to meet.

Our journey has been nothing short of magic. While reflecting on all that is contained in this book, I have to chuckle to myself because it is not hard to see the two different languages that we speak and why communication is not always easy. Communication is a skill developed, one that she is impeccable with and one in which I am very much still learning. To that she would say, impeccable or not, we are all always learning.

It is worthwhile to be truthful with ourselves about where we are at right now with no judgment, just clear honesty. While reading this book, the invitation is to be present, to feel what happens for you while you read and to approach those feelings with an intimate curiosity. Whatever it may be—a smile, a good cry, laughter or anger. Maybe it inspires you or reminds you of something on your own path. Look at it. See what's there, why it's there, and most importantly, where it is coming from.

A wonderfully wise and witty Lakota medicine man once showed me that we are only ever curious about what is in 'the bag' when we continue to show it off and talk about it. Once we know what is in there, we feel more at ease and not so drawn to 'the bag' anymore. I learned that we do this in our own bodies and minds, constantly telling a story about ourselves and others. Positive or negative, we feed these stories and thus keep holding on to our bags. Maybe it is our way of not wanting to let things or people go, so we do not have to be alone in this vast world. Or, maybe it is the idea that once we know what is in there, there would not be anything left for us to go on about. But I promise that once you know what is in your bags, you can move on to something newer and even more interesting. The rule of thumb is that there is always something that awaits us.

I would be remiss if I didn't leave you with one more thing that I have learned along my own path—take it for what it is worth. A dear friend of mine was absolutely right when he said that ice cream melts fast in the jungle. So, do not sell yourself short in pretending to only be a witness to what you are already so inclined to do. Engage. Be fully present. Be conscious. Be here.

This book is a conversation, a passing of letters, a myriad of collected experiences that thankfully words could be put to. As it often is with Pooja and I, you will find that we do not always adhere to conventional norms. In our writing, this could be perceived as a challenge to 'tradition' or as meaningful self-expression, or both. If we change who we are and how we express ourselves to fit in, where would that leave us in our commitment to soul?

We want you to understand that there is an incredibly deep ebb and flow of masculine and feminine energies amongst many other intricacies throughout the entirety of the book from cover to cover and that their significance stretches well beyond just the capitalizations or lack thereof of with words. Our message lies within the message. Don't (just) follow the words, follow the rhythm.

Some of these writings are newer and were written after we met one another, but most were written long before we found each other in this world. One of the more fascinating things is that when we got to talking about creating this book, we soon realized that we had both started writing this book around the same time as the other. Our work together started long before we met, long before we set foot on medicine journeys. It is likely that in those early moments, our path together was forged.

We do not really know who, where, when, and what is next for humanity, but an open curiosity and a willingness to abide by our own nature of being can keep us alert to what those things may be. The details are in our bodies, our minds, and our souls' scriptures. Listen for the next synchronicity. Listening, the first step in becoming a good communicator. Communication is a *massive* key, more important now than ever. All of our ancestors, no matter where they came from, sang, prayed, sat in ceremony, went through tough times, communicated and persevered. This is exactly why we are all here in the first place.

Lifetimes have passed since Pooja and I first met. I remember the sound of fire and water coming together in the womb of our very first temezcal ceremony. The sound produces a glimmer of a common language etched deep inside each and every one of our souls. From this sound emerges the idea that each element contains all of us and all of us are composed of the same elements. This movement, the precipice we all stand upon, truly takes each and every single one of us as individuals and as a part of the collective whole. Our contributions matter. It is so easy to remember this on our best days, but it is vital that we remember this during our darkest moments as well. This is why ceremony, prayer, listening and expression are where we so often turn to help us remember.

So, take hold of your sails and listen to the winds. A great fire is brewing, the waters are stirring, and the earth is calling us home. Here now, and until the end, we commit to praying, creating and learning together. We hope you enjoy this offering. We extend our gratitude to you and the fire you keep.

# CONTENTS

# HEALING

## *opening prayers*

we call in the direction of the east
where the sun rises with the gift of a new day
may we bow to the element of fire
and surrender to the alchemy of transformation
letting go, to let in

we call in the direction of the south
the element of air
may we harness the power of intention and vulnerability
as we speak our prayers into the winds
may we freely share our songs and receive each other's gifts with humbleness

we call in the direction of the west
the element of water
may we have the courage to feel
to stretch our hearts and let them break
to love ourselves and all there is without conditions or limits

we call in the direction of the north
the element of earth
may you help to ground and nourish us
teaching us to honor the inherent perfection and abundance within us
so we can honor and respect all the loving beings around us

## *opening prayers (continued)*

we honor the direction of above
grandfather sky
we ask that our ancestors, star families, angels and guides
all beings who come in unconditional love
protect us and guide us with power and grace

we honor the direction of below
grandmother earth
we invite her sacred medicines, plant, animal and beyond
to co-create with us in our healing and liberation

and finally,
we honor the direction of within
of sacred self

where heaven and earth,
masculine and feminine merge
where prophecies and dreams become reality
where we become one with ourselves,
and
all there is

## _to our loved ones who have transitioned_

for all the souls who walk the edge of darkness
thank you for your willingness
to carry us through remembrances of light
to whisper gently through our hearts
of our responsibility to living memories
we trust in your passing of the fire
receiving the torch with humility and gratitude
trusting further
that when you return
you will join us
in a season
in a spiral
closer to paradise

*cosmic wilderness*

the stars ripple off the moon,
she swallows a frog

the jaguar finds her tail,
gifting it to the light

while the gods of flowers remind us,
to 'drink the medicine'

## *I wish I knew what god was telling me*

I wish I knew what god was telling me
I wish I could be as still as the mountains
I wish I could let go like the leaves in the fall
I wish I could flow like the rivers that I cleanse in
I wish the trees would just pick me up and hold me
I wish to let go
I wish to let go
And all I can do is care
I walk to clear my head
And all I find are thoughts
Thoughts of this and thoughts of that
What is this silly game
Buddha says that all that we are is a result of our thinking
Then what have I become
In times like these I don't even know what to think
I've thought myself silly
I ask the trees "where do I go from here?"
Would you have guessed that they responded in silence
But there's so much work to do!
Go silent
Go silent
Go silent
They've figured out the game
How do I reach god when all these cares make me want to not care
Where is the sense?
And yet mountains go on being mountains and rivers as rivers
Clouds come and go and not a one dares to notice
The sun and the moon go on kissing and sharing light
And not a one realizes that they are the lifeline of all that we do
The trees go on reaching and rooting
And not a one stops to say hello
My cares are large and small alike
I sit
I sit and listen
What can I do?
Go on like everything else

*love letters from "c"*

**1. shadow teachings**
you know that relief you felt
when you heard the words
it's stage four
i felt it too
that was your soul,
beautiful one
that was your soul knowing
i'm here for a reason
that was your soul knowing
that everything is about to change
it'll be messy
it'll be painful
the loss, destruction, and death of the unhealed version of yourself
of who you thought you were
creating and birthing more beauty
than you could've ever imagined
if you can stay with me,
sit with me,
learn from me,
be with me,
i will help you
i will help you
i will help you
liberate your self
i will help you know
what is real and true
and release
what isn't worthy of you
—c.

_love letters from "c"_

## 2. listen here
your soul knows there are no accidents
only synchronicities
i am no accident
i am not to be conquered nor avoided
i am not evil
i come as your friend
i come as sacred messenger
love me, please
—c.

### 3. mind body soul
who am i?
you're one of the few brave enough to ask
i am many things
i am certainly not what they think—
careful what you tell them.

between me and you
i am a part of you in need of healing
this part of you is not just you
but a part of the whole that is in need
i am your ancestors in need of healing
your soul family
your birth family

i choose to live inside of you
because you, you, my dear
have the power to heal me
not just the power,
but the responsibility

healing me is a part of your greater purpose unfolding

you are not to blame for this dear one
be gentle with you
i know we can heal together
if i didn't believe in you,
i wouldn't be here
–c.

*love letters from "c"*

## 4. sovereignty
i am your
mother's trauma
that birthed you
suffocating
cord wrapped around your neck
on the cusp of life and death
it's time for you to
cut
the
c
o
r
d
s
once again
you are not your mother
you are not your mother's mother

find you.

and
breathe,
child.

cords are
only
as real
as you
make
them

trauma
is meant
to be healed

*love letters from "c"*

## 5. the end of the beginning
i am death
reminder and teacher of how to live
there is no need for fear
i am of the benevolent kind,
a temporary visitor.
i do not come empty handed,
i offer you
the
Unknown

*love letters from "c"*

## 6. de-programming
i am who you were
the one who thought
that in order to survive
she had to control,

to be someone else,
"he" maybe, him

the one with thick skin
no pain, no gain
strength in avoidance
what's the point in feeling?
show me the objective research.

experience is subjective and therefore meaningless, daughter.

look around,
logic is the way forward.

forget quantum – i'm talking linearity.
you command your body.
you conquer the mountain.
you compete, you capitalize,
you win.

it's called conditional love, baby.
opt in, and it will
destroy us all
you say you want to decolonize this planet?

start with yourself.

_love letters from "c"_

**7. radical acceptance**
i am neither your past nor your future
i am here, now
your highest, the highest

forgive me,
and i am yours.

ocean goddess
visionary healer
jaguar feeler
prophetess
medicine woman

be(lieve) me,
and i am yours.

## *Samsāra*

The sun shows everything for what it is. The moon shines a glimmer into what once was and what will be. Somewhere between I dwell within shadow and light. The stars remind me of an old memory that was never supposed to be remembered. Within my own eyes are endless stories and vast oceans where I sail to the darkest of waters and cast my line. On the bridge is where we watch all go by. Where could we possibly be in such deep spaces? What do we really hear, and what do we actually see when that line has been casted out so far? When there are no more questions being asked, there are no more answers to be delivered... Saṃsāra.

## _rose | thorn_

remember your soul chose your body
your melanin or lack thereof
your feminine, your masculine
and everything in between

remember your soul chose your blood
the ones who gave you life
their struggles and their sacrifices
their limitations and their liberations

remember your soul chose your light and your shadow
your grief and your joy
your heartbreaks and your loves
your bitter and your sweet

remember your soul chose these living paradoxes
to birth the uniqueness that is you
your special starseed offerings
that will save us all

remember,
in the end,
at the end,
your soul chose you.

## *Firekeeper*

The fire starts as a seed, fed by the broken and twisted fibers of the wood. This is a patient process, like the process of taking care of a plant. Does the fire start within the thought of the keeper or is its energy already inherent in its space? When is the child born? Through sitting and using the air from my lungs I am assisting in a tradition that has been going on for a long time. Through keeping the fire my ancestors are presently with me, a teaching passed on from the forefathers. With every fire lit across the earth the great stories of old are told, their voices carry through the wind like the flames carry through the intricate fibers of the wood. This is not something that should ever be lost. This is the solar energy manifested on earth, in our homes, in our places of prayer, in our hearts. Within the circle of light that is provided by the fire we are safe. With the fire we cook our delicious meals that nourish our bodies. The fire both destroys and forges, it is impeccably a symbol of the middle way. When does the fire start? And isn't it amazing that fire has the ability to turn people within? We are innately attracted to fire, this is where we gather, where we create, where we renew.

## _Two sides | One coin_

To sit with both God and Satan.
To walk with the sinners and sit with the saints.
The wholly other speaks in silence.
To see new things within the soul and only be sitting in your room.
Everywhere is your church.
Seeking is what they do and knowing is what I am not.
Speak of it and it's gone, think of it and it fades, hear it and it muffles...feel it and it is yours.
There is an old saying from the 'wisemen' of old... "when you really see it, you will laugh yourself silly."

## _nirvana_

the ugliest gifts are my greatest teachers
i bow to the poison within
even if it Kills me

### _dragonyoni_

fire breathing womb goddess, messages etched into her scales,
read the writing on her sacred walls
fear exists to be destroyed (and transformed)
shh, don't get ahead of yourself!
destruction happens first.
the will of the divine feminine is about balance,
not you.

it just _is._

blood,
birthing.
seeing,
knowing,
truthmaking.

do not underestimate the power of our tears and our screams
our bodies were born to move rage like pristine oceanwaves
powerfully gentle
disruptively peaceful
mysterious, transparent
we cannot be controlled.

you will remember this,
when the flames rip through your vessels
you will remember this,
when fire finds its way into your bones
you will remember this,
when heat discovers the taste of your blood
and
shreds it all to ash.

dragonyonis,
let our collective angers flow
and show ourselves what we already know
some things are meant to be incinerated.

## *The Blue Flower*

The blue flower stands at the edge of space. It is a ceremonial flower and the gateway has opened like a lotus. Ri Ren as my great teacher would say. The realm of plant medicine runs deep and I am a shaman, exploring the etheric fluids of the deep womb of existence. Tomorrow is just another day crashing into shore and yesterday was swept under by the waves. Right now, right here, this side of the island is well kept and all is well underneath the starry gaze of that holy(wholly) other who is looking in through my vehicle. I am an explorer. Beauty recognizes beauty. Up the staircase I tread lightly in the steps of my forefathers.

### _why i heal_

i heal for myself
and i heal for you
i heal for my children
and i heal for yours too

i heal for my ancestors
and those we share
i heal for the earth
and our collective despair

i heal for the water
and i heal for the sand
i heal for the creatures
walking with us hand in hand

i heal for liberation
the place where our souls connect
i heal for reimagination
the space where our dreams intersect

*to heal or not to heal?*

for some it presents as a question
a soft knock
at the door
for others it's a loud scream
a womxn drowning
heard from shore
for me
it was the latter
near death in the open sea
to ignore her cries
meant goodbye
that is how healing called me

## *intuition*

there i was
treading to survive
drained and depleted
trying to stay alive

a tiny hummingbird
it heard my pleas
and so she came
flying with ease

her energy was fierce
movements joyful and sweet
she arrived with a stone
and a familiar *geet*

she let the stone drop
and as i watched it fall
let go, she said
once and for all

let go? no way!
that's for the weak
stubborn, i was
trapped in my critique

let go, she insisted
the goddess inside me
as water filled my lungs
i knew it was the key

note: *geet* (hindi) means 'song'

## *letting go*

i let myself journey
into the darkness that resides
into the rage and the sorrow
and the hatred that divides

i stepped into the trauma
i feared for so long
terrified i would never return
if i really listened to its song

i heard our children's screams
bodies taken without consent
i heard the cries of stolen earth
and centuries of discontent

i heard my own shame
could i have done more?
i questioned my worth
what am i truly good for?

yet the more i surrendered
to the hurt deep inside
i found we could hang
two dost, side by side

note: *dost* (hindi) means 'friend'

*rest*

i took another breath
welcomed the darkness once more,
that's when i learned
not everything has to feel like war

from fighting to floating
i rest with sea,
dreaming of the hummingbird
coming back to me

## _The Quest Within_

One finds themself with a question, "the question," or, many questions. So we start our trek up the mountain with backpack on our shoulders. As we climb higher and higher, we find ourselves shedding things from our pack, or parts of our identity. The details are in the mountain and we spend many a days going through different terrain and wonderful weather. We climb higher and higher. Eventually along the way, we completely forget the question on this journey but recognize that we have come so far—so we must keep going. We finally reach the top and enter into the cave of the guru, only to find that the guru is self and that there is no question. The only thing left to do is is sit with the guru within. I find mySelf on this mountain. I have been shedding things from my pack, I have forgotten my question and I feel close to the guru at the top. What or who will be there when I arrive and what will come after is a mystery of the divine that I will soon realize.

*witness*

himá
ā-laya
snow dwelling.
under the blankets of snow
live Rocks

billions, probably
one on top of another
existing imperfectly in all their dimensions
a sort of peaceful discomfort
rough edges neighboring one another
a Family,
a people

jagged
Disruptive
disrupted

Organized

into
Mountains.
colossal and immovable
try to take, to build, to unearth, to break
Her
you can try
yet,

*witness (continued)*

we are still.
present.
still present.
the universe itself resides in us,
in our Memories
ask us anything

we have seen Everything you wonder,
but cannot Touch
we have lived Stories who find refuge
in the spaces between the tiny cracks
of our palms
that you sometimes trace
                        with your footsteps

the same palms of the familiar hands
colored with soil,
color of soil
that welcome me back
with a small cup of steaming chai

the same hands
whose fingertips release
the invisible ivy coiled around my earthfeet
as she whispers to my toetips
speaking to the question
i didn't even know i had

            'this is the place your soul resides
                        before they came and after they left'

## _Not so alone after all_

The shaman's path. My brother's keeper. I keep a watchful eye on my tribe. Everyone is accounted for. I stay back. I am a warrior. I am a lone wolf, but always accompanied by the pack. I am the mystic. I know magic and I am sitting on the cusp of the doorway. On the other side I do not know what awaits me, but I must go. This is different this time around. I often forget just how deep it really goes. The journey. The path I walk is a lonesome one and yet I am never truly alone. It is a warrior's path. A shaman's path. My friends are out there, the fellowship is real. The flame is still, the moment of initiation has begun. A break in the realms is coming, a break through the ethers. A drumming on the wind.

## *seven generations*

the cracks of hardened blood
lay thick on the skin of our hearts
our collective womb seared
with the genocide of sovereignty

soul. body. land. breath.

the flames of rage ravage our earth bodies
channeling waves of destruction
genocide breeds suicide,
death.

let them burn.
let us burn.
let us honor the sacred fires of protection
moving our cells to shake with grief

shake moving shake
breathe easy baby

let us hold our ancestors through the pain
until their ashes touch the hearts of whiteness
loosening the coils of hatred wrapped around our throats
prison bars caging our pussy

until we can breathe
breathe easy
breathe easy baby

the whole of our bodies knowing the truth
of our children's children's children's children's children's children's children
seven generations to infinity
resting peacefully in the golden light of divine love
the sparkling waters of boundless grace
the refreshing airs of purity and innocence
and the sacred fires of divine justice.

# TRANSITIONS

### *when i lost you*

when i lost you i had already lost myself,
rather
what i thought
was me

i had died hadn't i?

i can't tell you what it felt like to lose you afterwards
because i didn't feel it

feeling meant
choosing death again

i chose to survive.

i held on to your remains
a survival secret of mine
hollowed out,
dried blood and bones
turned to ash

at least then all of you wouldn't be lost

i carried what was left of you in a small bag
inside an endless dark hole carved with blades of ice and fire
deep within my core
a breathtaking tapestry
made blank

erased,
but not gone.

## _our darkness is our humanity_

resentment
the feeling of not being heard, understood or seen
let feeling live in your body for too long and it gets crusty and scars over

at least scars are visible.

age old memories of being shoved into boxes you didn't choose to be in
not quite the décor you would have chosen, nor the shape – obviously.
who wants to be imprisoned forever?

hurt underneath layers of more hurt
that may never be heard
no matter how loud we scream

where and how do we place it nice and neat so it doesn't hurt anyone's feelings?

let's launder our hurt. Clean it, fold it and organize it
so it doesn't seem so cruel.
Forcing ourselves to sanitize our hurt IS.
is Violence.

when did we start being so ashamed of our darkness?

## *Bugaboo buzz buzz*

Up here I cease to exist. What is that buzzing around? Why come and see! It must be me! But where to start? Where to look? For it doesn't matter I am not there. Float float floating away. Chirpity chirp, knock knock knocked. Am I looking out at myself or am I looking into myself? Breathe in breathe out. Death, life, death, life. Cyclic tuning for that brave star seed. Boom! For out of nothing can't come something! For there had to be something all along. Big bang theory is only a theory for those that meddle with questions that will never have answers. State your status captain for we are ready to fly. Hum hum hummingbird for I wish I could keep up; your very nature keeps me on my toes in a cosmic chase through time. For what is time without a watch? Aha out here we are eternal. For what is anything without measurement? Aha so there is where we cease to exist. But here I am, humbled and arrogant all at once. For I know nothing and yet believe that I do. Aha madness is standing on that edge knowing you could fall but knowing you won't. State your status captain for we are only ever a moment away at all times from knowing something we already know but are only pretending that we don't. To know that you don't know is indeed stating that you know. Beautiful. Wonderful. Cosmic befundering.

### _mapping magic_

my ancestors always say
she lives in between _between_ spaces :
visit the formed yet unbroken wave
and you might even catch a sighting
dolphinbirds dancing
tunes of griefjoy and more
swirling and twirling through homecomings of abundant abundance
let yourself feel into the starscapes
where ancient dreams of now manifest
in body, embodied,
somewhere after ocean ends
before it transforms
into sky

## *White Shore*

Water drifting turns rock to sand, a seed from a tree goes running by. Beneath is above as up is below, time complacency is an error in way. Endless doors come turning up, through which ghosts of past and souls of new await within. On this bridge we all pass, some will know and some need time. If I could show you what I know then you wouldn't worry about what it is that you don't know. My message lies within the message, it follows me as I walk. I see a song and I feel a color, don't follow the words but follow the rhythm. What do you see when you look again? Feet on the ground and head in the stars, body between doing bodily things. When one says, "I know," what do they know? Kaleidoscope hyperbolic geometry, patterns all around. Interconnected waters and all passing through. These are some things that happen when we pull away the veil. A walk around the world is no walk at all, it is a ceremony where all souls pass.

## *let it burn*

as you become you
people fall away
sometimes gently
like leaves on an autumn day
other times with more force
trees engulfed by forest flames
either way
what's gone is gone
what's dead is dead
it must be so,
and it still hurts
grieve the ones you've lost,
but don't lose yourself in your grief
as your reality dissolves
your roots grow stronger
the fire burns, hotter and hotter
until it reaches the optimal temperature
in this divinely scheduled time,
thousands of seedlings are birthed
from inside of you
now, amidst the destruction
there is plenty of space for light and water
to reach sacred new life
waiting to be born

## _The truth in the brandywine_

The wind blows and the trees sway
The river flows and I sit
The bubbles of the river surface to the water, the moment doesn't falter
And I sit
The leaf dances while the spider weaves,
The fox plays while the deer are at ease
There is a universe, just look and see
Through our eyes are endless seas whispering lightly of timeless tales
There is a moment that never fails
And I sit...do you see?

*to the keepers of the light*

just as we built our own cages
so too we hold the keys
for our own liberation

## *wild grace: a manifesto*

i freely choose to follow the deepest Callings of my soul

should these Callings guide me to let go
of relationships, commitments, feelings or mindsets
let it be so

should these Callings guide me to leave home
in search of something i feel but cannot explain
let it be so

should my truth bring anyone discomfort,
including myself,
let it be so

i repeat:
let it be so

should fear kick in,
may i remember that love rules
and abundance is god's law

Love rules.
Abundance is God's law.

should evil seem to prevail,
may i remember that i am a warrior
that it is my responsibility to speak out, rebel and refuse
and that the fires of divine justice stand with me

i repeat:
i am a warrior.
the fires of divine justice stand with me.

## *wild grace: a manifesto (continued)*

should i forget who i am or why i am here
may i have the strength to ask for help
to sit, to pray, to dance, to sing
to commune with mother earth,
until i remember

Sit, pray, dance, sing.
Commune with Mother Earth.
Until We Remember.

# LIBERATION

## *Eternal love flame*

There are infinite forms of love. The love that you know today will soon be an old form and will be replaced by a higher and more updated version of love. And all of it is love, but one must be willing to die over and over again within the fire to ultimately come to their own understanding that the very fire they died in is the very fire they arose in. It's all love. It's just a journey deeper and deeper within, because what you love in another is also within you, what you find beautiful in another is the same beauty within you. It is an awareness and a remembering of the wholeness that is already present. To the fire and back, eternity lives.

## _whole stove kisses_

and just when eyes moonlight
    touch listens
whole water attractions.
        like fingers across
            somehow.

           up lights literal being
              lighting soul

                and be from body like
       butterflies afloat

           soft piano earth
aware. me
    their divine
        like
          long
             knowing
               moonlight

## _melanated love_

her long hands cup my chin gingerly
as our lips meet

my fingertips glide across her arms
dancing delicately to debussy

it's the golden hour

under the magic of the evening sky
my breath is heavy and deep

tickling the chrysanthemums
snow-white blooms swaying gently

to the sweet song of melanated love

## _abuela mariposa_

walking in the forest,
the butterfly finds you
orange and purple,
grey with tinges of blue ocean
sprinkles of angel white,
dots of red earth

you think to yourself,
how did pachamama create something so beautiful?

you are the butterfly, and
the butterfly is you

your grandmother resides in her wings
she lifts the grief from your heart
tickling your soul with nourishment and grace
reminding you it is okay to come out of your cocoon
from time to time
to fly

to fly over the trees and amongst them
to fly over the rivers and streams
to fly amongst the birds and the bees

and sometimes,
to simply,
rest on a leaf
and
dream

## *Grandfather Kapok*

At the top of the Kapok tree, I ascended and sat with my grandfather. There he smiled his playfully mischievous and memorable smile. Not a word was said but a profound feeling ran its course through this experience. To understand the generational line, the ancestral line that runs through my blood and through the DNA of myself and all of my relations. All of the time, the energy, the effort that brings to life the existence of me and all others.

A tree begins as a seed, then the roots form, then it reaches for light and begins its trunk, and then the leaves begin and finally the fruits of its labor...only to disperse them around and start again. Humans are no different than this, nothing is different than this. All of existence is doing this. The universe continues to provide so as to keep itself flowing, expanding and alive.

My grandfather taught me true friendship, he taught me how to play, and in the end, he taught me how important it is to take care of our elders. Because arms we were once carried and cherished in as children become the arms that we must in return carry and cherish as the ones that came before us become older.

His most important teaching came when his tree no longer stood above ground...it's that all things never die, that his creation came long before and the fruits of his life are all around in the form of his children, his friends, his connections. Through memory and time, we must witness a passing of a myriad of things, but they never die. My grandfather taught me patience in a time of the world and in a culture that lacks it. To take time in the smallest of things because they become the biggest of things. What runs through you and I is a force and a power that is so strong it cannot be broken.

Take care of the mind, it is a great servant but a bad master. Take care of the body, this is what your soul uses to explore its existence and it is the greatest gift spirit has given us. Flow like the water, carry like the wind, forge yourself in the fire and burn what isn't needed, and be strong like the mother, the earth. I will be there when the work is done. What will I leave for my grandchildren?

## *playtime*

i sent my sis some books
they got lost in the mail

what if they went to jupiter?
what a long way to sail

i ventured out there
into clouds of ammonia

wearing my special suit
lower risk of pneumonia!

without a solid surface
i kinda lost my way

thank god she found me
sis wanted to play

we bounced on liquid crystal
in tropical region four

and danced so hard
we needed an encore...

## *Slithered Water*

I casted your lifeless body down river, intuitively knowing you would return full of life. For water is the bearer of life. Water is healing. It is the clear liquid light of the mother goddess. I sent you down river, dear serpent. I could not allow your body to be neighbored by busy-ness. It was only right to give you back to the mother and her sweet waters. You have returned in good timing, dear serpent. Kundalini rises. The kundalini energies are stirring and spiraling up and down. Time to enter into the eternal timeless of all. You gracefully glide through the waters and come to the shore where I reside. You come bearing messages from spirit, from the ether. Worship the goddess and the crownless will be king. Serpent, you are the epitome of keeping the body still and yet it looks and seems as if you are moving. For you are moving, it is the mind, it is the energy. Rise kundalini. Rise spiraling quintessence. Rise. There is nothing to fear, enter through the gates and drink the sweet liquid light of the mother and claim the throne. It is birthright. Trust like the bird landing on a branch. Move swift like the wind. I am strong in my fluidity. I am fluid in my strength. Just like the serpent, I rise. I am rise.

## creatrix codes

our flow is advanced magic
this ain't no beginner's dance
wild love sorcery
creating life, death

transmuting collective agony
beauty, power, wisdom, compassion

we are the feminine force

whispering winds
uprooting lava
sounding thunder
making waves

this is us

feeling is healing
feeling is queen-ing

honor the bleed
remembering the gifts of our ancients
dripping down lineage
the divine feminine creatrix codes

the sacred way.
the only way.

breathe. rest. protect.
the sacred passageway

the original creatrix matrix
*this* is our medicine

_the water dances_

sacred union:
through union we heal
transform, die
and sometimes agree to do it all over again

    nothing is mandatory in life except death

        let's dance with the fire
              by the fire
              in the fire
          we are the fire

        let's dance with the fire
              by the fire
              in the fire
          we are the fire

        let's dance with the fire
              by the fire
              in the fire
          we are the fire

    remembering pachamama has all the ingredients we need for liberation

drum it in.
drum it out.
stomp it in.
stomp it out.
dance it dance it dance it.
beat it.
drum it.
beat it.
|| || ||| || ||||

        save yourself
          then,
      let's walk home together

## *The Edge*

On the edge. Aren't we always on the edge? Have I not written about the edge before? Barefoot and I love it. Feet in direct contact with the mother, pulses being sent between the two. Pulses of love and health and being. Ancestral bodies sprouting all around. A lineage I walk and hope to live up to. Sitting long enough, doesn't it always seem that the environment comes to you after you come to it? Stream and river merge. The water from the high mountains and hills is now exalted from its duty. It has done the work to come far through land and rock and trees. In ecstasy it is released into the river. More work to be done, but much closer to source. The source. Isn't that what we all are doing? I will continue to put my feet on the earth, doing my work, in hopes of drawing closer to home. Journey on my brothers and sisters. I am thankful and I am blessed.

## *god | us*

trust in god
trust in ourselves

when we trust in ourselves
we trust in god
we trust in each other

faith flowers
we don't need proof

we dance it in our feet
we smell it in our bones
we weave it our blood

we see the window
we take it
we feel the path
we walk it

this
is how
we make it

## _Elemental healing_

The water cleanses me
The trees teach me
The earth grounds me
And the air fills me up

## _sacred stuff_

hear the whispers of our womb
under the guise of the moon

my blood chooses peace
my water wholeness
my being, life

inhale | exhale
every breath is sacred

inhale | exhale
our womb is sacred

## *Waking Lessons*

It is always right here in the present, where truth, beauty and wholeness reside. Words don't do it justice. It is a feeling. An experience felt. How often it is forgotten among many. How often it is that I forget. How humbling it is to remember. The serpent returns. Kundalini has been activated. The wholly other showed me that. This, I believe is why my sexual energy has been stirring so much. This, I feel, is a great source of knowledge and with action behind knowledge, it becomes wisdom. Felt wisdom. Alchemy. This is a narrow path indeed. How easy it is to be pulled off the path. Stay to the path. Stay to the disciplines. Remembering to remind...Reminding to remember. I am on the forged path. I am strong. God is here at all times, with me, the kingdom is inside. The juice of the gods has been served. God, Satan, the angels, archangels and I-self-dweller all sit at the table and discuss matters of light and dark. All context, All union. The heart center is stimulated, let's continue the good work. Thank you, God, for the reminder that this path is narrow and that it is one well worth walking. Ri Ren.

### <u>*dance with me*</u>

dance with me
kiss my breasts with your lips
let them nourish you with earth
while my sacred waters
flow unto your heart
expansive and expanding,
opening
our collective breaths
lighting the fire of our y/noni spirits
dance with me baby
that true shamanic dance
dance into my cosmic womb
till we're home sweet home
the truth of god
resting in our fingertips

## _Dwelling Star_

When the final note has played on our physical existence, what have you brought? How did you greet yourself in the mirror during those mornings? How did you carry yourself throughout your days? What did you learn? What did you say? What did I teach you? I know what you have taught me. There is no death, there is no end...you and I go dancing eternally as friends. We have met before and we will meet again. There is no worry on this man's end. We've watched it all come and go...how do we fulfill our status quo? You walk upon land that is shared with all...who is really to determine who should stay and who should go. I walk the trails that are back home and have shared a thought or two with the trees that accompany me to the end. They have heard my prayers and casted them into the river only to find myself among the mountains. The higher you climb the closer you get to yourself. My words don't have to travel as far as I am close to the heavens. I feel your prayers and I see your faces...we are not alone but close together. The night is telling and from the star that guards the bear is where you can always find me. I walk the path of the wolf, sometimes lone but always a part of the pack. The song has been sung and my only task is to keep the fire...for as long as it is lit you will always know where to find me. What will be your final message amidst the flash that is your life? And can you hear that beautiful melody in the air that is emanating from you?

## *sing with me*

sing with me
honoring the original flower
the force of cosmic creation
yes, sing her your truest songs
sweeter than nectar
slowly and gently
as she blossoms into ceremonial blessings
for our starscape reunion

## *Primal flux*

Shed...shed, shed, and shed again until
there isn't anything left except for who you really are.
Primordial freedom is inevitable.

## _dream with me_

dream with me
can we bury ourselves with grace
dancing into death
praying as we perish
unto heaven on earth?

## _Psilotales_

The Holy other. Time folds backwards and collapses into itself. Unto itself. The spiraling staircase. Winding on and on. The man holding the hand of a child. Guiding the child is the father's duty. The man and the child are one and the same. The light at the end of the spiraling tunnel. Winding up and down the spinal cord of evolution. Ancestral coding, tapping into genetic wisdom, cellular power. The hour, minute, and second hand of the clock spiraling up and down the nervous system. Re-coding and downloading. The digital rubix cube flowing like water, flashes of holy remembrance. The formless and forceful ancient entity wanting to be known. Inside the timeless void and traveling through hyperspace. Speaking in tongue and singing all fear and anxiety completely away. All that remains is healing, health, bravery, magic, knowing, joy and love. I am the program and I am the programmer. Flower of life showing all reference points and cross-referencing maps of reality, maps of programming, maps of consciousness. Grandfather sun, Grandmother moon, Father sky, Mother earth. Water bearer, fire conjurer, earth shifter, air bender. The timeless, eternal and immortal.

### _an infinity prayer_

teach me how to love you
teach me how to love me
how far can we stretch our hearts?
how much can we feel them break?
infinite compassion, infinite love
this is my prayer

∞

## _Hoodakai_

Came from the stars.
Inhabited the mountains.
Guardian of the earth mother.
Keeper of the fire.
Tongue of the winds.
Movement of the waters.
Traveler of all dimensions.
Woooosh.

## *paradox*

myself as me
what I thought I wanted was a safe love
safety,
a desired cage. a haven of sorts
peace | chaos
remember when we felt safe in the arms of pachamama? in her womb?
the same pachamama who reminds us that to love is to feel unsafe
will they hurt me?
will they kill me?
AM. I. SAFE.


history repeats itself and it doesn't
we seek to break her cycle,
yet we seek familiarity


the edge.


are you open to it?
let go


let go
beyond the shadows of doubt and fear
play it safe and we go nowhere


too dangerous and …
love is a dangerous game
where there lies a new haven, a true haven


hold my hand dear friend, dear stranger,
and let's fall dangerously
together

## _A drumming upon the winds_

I saw you in the black of night.
And you saw me in the darkest knight.
The virtuous light of truth came penetrating through as the quiet jaguar listened
and opened doorway
Hawk soars and lion roars
Mountain quests and ocean depths
I came to you in the black of night
And you taught me things of inherent birthright
Jungle visions and strong allegiances
These are times of great awakenings
These are times of revolutions
These are times of tribe gatherings
These are times that the narrow path is narrowing
These are times we must put away the differences
These are times we must be listening
These are times we must be sharing
Archer stance and keep your glance
Straight as an arrow
There may not be a tomorrow
I heard the voices come sifting through the deepest jungles
And I heard the drumming come upon four winds

## _naked_

love,
we did it for you.
shame has no place
in our womb
little one,
we did it for you.
see your mama and papa
in their sacred sensuality
she burns, a phoenix
he breathes, a dragon
soft and gentle, a dove
in their eyes you see the truth of the unmasking
unmaking,
of generations
the unraveling of sacrifice into blankets of innocence
as light as air
may you, little one, fly freely into yourself
may you feel the gifts of your soul body
like infinite spheres of rose gold and cobalt blue
intertwining into a radiant amethyst purple
threading your y/noni,
with your heart,
to your crown
and beyond
may you, little one,
be free

### *soulspeak, a closing prayer*

listen
take my words as truth
take my words as prayer
as song
listen to my voice as you do wind and fire
my words matter
listen before you speak
let my words seep into your blood and your bones
feel compassion
feel, me

xx
your be-loved soul

# ABOUT THE AUTHORS

**Pooja Bakhai** is the first of two daughters born to Indian parents on Iroquois land. Pooja means 'sacred ceremony' in Gujarati, Hindi and Sanskrit. Pooja is a spiritual guide, forever student, and divine channel for dance, song and prayer. Pooja's mission is to support her community in their quest for liberation with love, realness and a dash of spice.

**Matthew Steele** was born and raised by the Brandywine Valley, original and native land to the Lenape peoples. Matthew means 'gift of God, gift of Yahweh' in Hebrew. Matthew is of Irish, Scottish, German, British and Cherokee descent, amongst other lineages. He is a healer, medicine man, an explorer of consciousness and life, and lover of simple things.

Any comments and inquiries kindly send to cosmicwildernessfam@gmail.com

Made in the USA
Middletown, DE
16 November 2023